Published in 2005 by

Stewart, Tabori & Chang, 115 West 18th Street, New York, NY 10011
www.abramsbooks.com

Library of Congress Cataloging-in-Publication Data
Montrose, Sharon.
Dachshunds : lightweights-littermates / Sharon Montrose.
p. cm.
ISBN 1-58479-468-2
1. Dachshunds—Pictorial works. I. Title
SF429.D25M66 2005
636.753'8—dc22
2005042606

Designed by Sally Ann Field
Production by Alexis Mentor

The text of this book was composed in Eatwell Skinny & Eatwell Chubby by Chank Diesel.

Printed in China

10 9 8 7 6 5 4 3 2

Stewart, Tabori & Chang is a subsidiary of

LA MARTINIÈRE
GROUPE